Plants

Plant Math

Patricia Whitehouse

Heinemann Library
Chicago, Illinois

Customer Service 888-454-2279
Visit our website at www.heinemannlibrary.com

Designed by Sue Emerson/Heinemann Library, Page layout by Carolee A. Biddle
Printed and bound in the U.S.A. by Lake Book

06 05 04 03 02
10 9 8 7 6 5 4 3 2 1

Library of Congress Cataloging-in-Publication Data
Whitehouse, Patricia, 1958-
    Plant math / Patricia Whitehouse.
        p. cm. — (Plants)
Includes index.
Summary: A counting book featuring various plants.
    ISBN 1-58810-523-7 (HC), 1-58810-734-5 (Pbk.)
    1. Counting—Juvenile literature. 2. Plants—Juvenile literature. [1.
Counting. 2. Plants.] I. Title. II. Plants (Des Plaines, Ill.)
    QA113 .W495 2002
    513.2'11—dc21
    [[2001003719

Acknowledgments
The author and publishers are grateful to the following for permission to reproduce copyright material:
p. 3 Jerome Wexler/Visuals Unlimited; pp. 5, 22, 23B, 24 Dwight Kuhn; p. 7 Wally Eberhart/Visuals Unlimited; pp. 9, 13 Amor Montes De Oca; pp. 11, 17, 19 Rick Wetherbee; p. 15 Rob and Ann Simpson; p. 21 E. R. Degginger/Color Pic, Inc.; p. 23T Joe McDonald/McDonald Wildlife Photography

Cover photographs courtesy of (L–R): Jerome Wexler/Visuals Unlimited; Dwight Kuhn; Rick Wetherbee

Every effort has been made to contact copyright holders of any material reproduced in this book.
Any omissions will be rectified in subsequent printings if notice is given to the publisher.

Special thanks to our advisory panel for their help in the preparation of this book:
Eileen Day, Preschool Teacher
Chicago, IL

Paula Fischer, K–1 Teacher
Indianapolis, IN

Sandra Gilbert,
Library Media Specialist
Houston, TX

Angela Leeper,
Educational Consultant
North Carolina Department
of Public Instruction
Raleigh, NC

Pam McDonald, Reading Teacher
Winter Springs, FL

Melinda Murphy,
Library Media Specialist
Houston, TX

Helen Rosenberg, MLS
Chicago, IL

Anna Marie Varakin,
Reading Instructor
Western Maryland College

The publishers would also like to thank Anita Portugal, a master gardener at the Chicago Botanic Garden, for her help in reviewing the contents of this book for accuracy.

Some words are shown in bold, **like this.**
You can find them in the picture glossary on page 23.

One 1

1

Seeds grow in the ground.

Count the seeds you see here.

Two   2

Roots grow in the ground.

Count the roots you
see here.

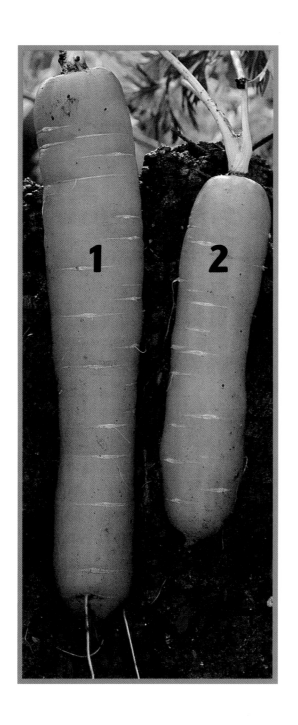

Three 3

Leaves grow on plants.

Count the leaves you see here.

1

2

3

Four 4

Flowers grow on plants.

Count the flowers you see here.

Five 5

Rabbits eat leaves and **roots.**

Count the roots you see here.

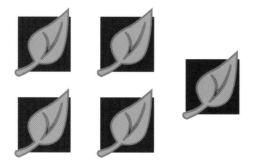

Six　6

People eat **roots**.

Count the radish roots you see here.

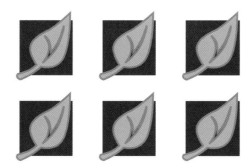

Seven 7

Birds eat seeds.

Count the birds you see here.

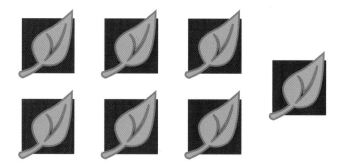

Eight 8

Bees drink **nectar** from flowers.

Count the flowers you see here.

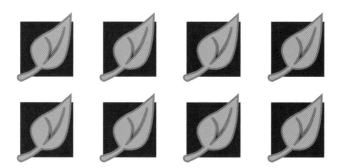

Nine   9

People grow flowers to give as presents.

Count the flowers you see in this present.

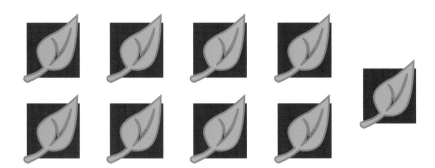

Ten 10

People plant seeds to grow flowers and vegetables.

Count the groups of seeds you see here.

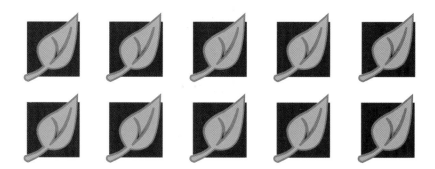

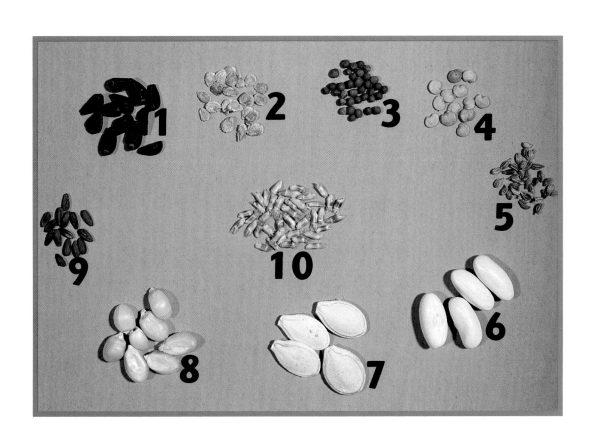

Look Closely!

How many seeds do you see?

Look for the answer on page 24.

Picture Glossary

nectar
page 16

root
pages 4–5,
    10–11, 12–13

23

Note to Parents and Teachers

Using this book, children can practice basic mathematical skills while learning interesting facts about plants. Help children see the relationship between the numerals 1 through 10 and the leaf icons at the bottom of each text page. Extend the concept by drawing ten "leaves" on a sheet of construction paper. Cut out the paper leaves. Together, read *Plant Math,* and as you do so, ask the child to place the appropriate number of "leaves" on the photograph. This activity can also be done using manipulatives such as dried beans or bay leaves.

Index

Answer to quiz on page 22
There are ten seeds in the beans.

24